A Firefighter's Story

Copyright © 2017 by Scott Finazzo

All rights reserved.

Cover design by Scott Finazzo / Pixelstudio
Book design concept by Scott Finazzo

No part of this book may be reproduced in any form or by any electronic or mechanical means, including information storage and retrieval systems, without permission in writing from the author.

www.scottfinazzo.com
Printed in the United States of America

A Firefighter's Story

Throughout your career you will collect an abundance of stories: some funny, some heroic, and of course, some tragic. You don't have to work this job very long before they begin to accumulate. Structure fires, traumatic scenes, extreme weather, firehouse antics, and countless other events take up real estate inside of us. It is those events that make up the fabric of the profession you have chosen: a firefighter.

I have spent many years writing in various journals and for a variety of reasons. None of them, though, were specific to what we do. I wanted to create a journal specifically for firefighters. The purpose of this journal is for it to be whatever you need it to be. It could be a place to document your chosen path of public safety. It could be a safe haven for you to unload your victories and heartbreaks, your fears and goals. Some may choose to keep a daily account of their life on shift while others may simply document remarkable occurrences. My hope is this journal becomes whatever you need it to become.

The benefits of keeping a journal are many. In his book *Writing to Heal*, Dr. James Pennebaker states, "When we translate an experience into language, we essentially make the experience graspable." Study after study has shown that keeping a journal can lower stress, reduce anxiety, evoke mindfulness, and even increase the likelihood of achieving goals by writing them down.

Journaling can help clarify thoughts and feelings as well as chronicle all the incidents and emotions that you will process day to day as a firefighter.

This book is your story.

How to Use This Journal

Journals can be daunting. A seemingly endless sea of blank lines in which you are expected to fill with profound words lies in front of you. I want to change that mindset. In this journal, each entry is divided into two pages. The first page is broken up into four categories:

What is the Best Thing That Happened Today?
This section is reserved for the moment or moments in a day that you identify as those that brought you joy. Write about a call, a funny event, a leadership moment, or a memorable quote. Over the course of any given day there are moments, both big and small, that deserve to be acknowledged. Seek out those happy moments and write them here.

What Troubled Me Today?
In this space, you can write what happened during the day that troubled you or that you wish you could do differently. Did you make a mistake? Did you have a disagreement with someone on your shift? Is something going on in your life outside of work that is bothersome? Some days this event or events could be the same thing that you've already addressed, but other days there will be distinct differences. Use this field to write what is weighing most on your mind.

What Am I Grateful For Today?
Gratitude is such an important part of a healthy outlook and positive state of mind. You should find items every day for which to be grateful. Identify people, moments, traits, or any number of other things that bring joy into your life. Again, even though this is a firefighter journal, your life outside of the station certainly can and should be included here.

How Can I Be Better Tomorrow?
Rarely do we make major changes over the course of a single day, but determining ways that you can improve your job skills, leadership qualities, life habits, and any other way that you can improve yourself as a person and as a firefighter should go here. It can certainly be big picture improvements, but can also be the tiniest areas of growth that will make you a better firefighter and happier person. This is a good place to document your goals. Challenge yourself to find ways to grow every day.

The second page is for you to document, vent, create, draw, or any combination of those. Use it however you need. Do not limit yourself to the space available on that page. If your entry rolls over onto the following page or pages, that's great. Don't stop the process.

DATE: _____ CREW: _____
WEATHER: _____ _____
STATION: _____ _____
UNIT: _____ _____

WHAT WAS THE BEST PART OF MY DAY?

WHAT TROUBLED ME TODAY?

WHAT AM I GRATEFUL FOR TODAY?

HOW CAN I BE BETTER TOMORROW?

DATE: _____ CREW: _____
WEATHER: _____ _____
STATION: _____ _____
UNIT: _____ _____

WHAT WAS THE BEST PART OF MY DAY?

_____
_____
_____
_____
_____
_____

WHAT TROUBLED ME TODAY?

_____
_____
_____
_____
_____
_____

WHAT AM I GRATEFUL FOR TODAY?

_____
_____
_____
_____
_____
_____

HOW CAN I BE BETTER TOMORROW?

_____
_____
_____
_____
_____
_____

DATE: _____ CREW: _____
WEATHER: _____ _____
STATION: _____ _____
UNIT: _____ _____

WHAT WAS THE BEST PART OF MY DAY?

_____
_____
_____
_____
_____
_____

WHAT TROUBLED ME TODAY?

_____
_____
_____
_____
_____
_____

WHAT AM I GRATEFUL FOR TODAY?

_____
_____
_____
_____
_____
_____

HOW CAN I BE BETTER TOMORROW?

_____
_____
_____
_____
_____
_____

DATE: _____   CREW: _____
WEATHER: _____   _____
STATION: _____   _____
UNIT: _____   _____

WHAT WAS THE BEST PART OF MY DAY?

WHAT TROUBLED ME TODAY?

WHAT AM I GRATEFUL FOR TODAY?

HOW CAN I BE BETTER TOMORROW?

DATE: _____ CREW: _____
WEATHER: _____ _____
STATION: _____ _____
UNIT: _____ _____

WHAT WAS THE BEST PART OF MY DAY?

_____
_____
_____
_____
_____
_____

WHAT TROUBLED ME TODAY?

_____
_____
_____
_____
_____
_____

WHAT AM I GRATEFUL FOR TODAY?

_____
_____
_____
_____
_____
_____

HOW CAN I BE BETTER TOMORROW?

_____
_____
_____
_____
_____
_____

DATE: _____ CREW: _____
WEATHER: _____ _____
STATION: _____ _____
UNIT: _____

WHAT WAS THE BEST PART OF MY DAY?

_____
_____
_____
_____
_____

WHAT TROUBLED ME TODAY?

_____
_____
_____
_____
_____

WHAT AM I GRATEFUL FOR TODAY?

_____
_____
_____
_____
_____

HOW CAN I BE BETTER TOMORROW?

_____
_____
_____
_____
_____

DATE: CREW:
WEATHER:
STATION:
UNIT:

WHAT WAS THE BEST PART OF MY DAY?

WHAT TROUBLED ME TODAY?

WHAT AM I GRATEFUL FOR TODAY?

HOW CAN I BE BETTER TOMORROW?

DATE: _____   CREW: _____
WEATHER: _____   _____
STATION: _____   _____
UNIT: _____   _____

WHAT WAS THE BEST PART OF MY DAY?

_____
_____
_____
_____
_____
_____

WHAT TROUBLED ME TODAY?

_____
_____
_____
_____
_____
_____

WHAT AM I GRATEFUL FOR TODAY?

_____
_____
_____
_____
_____
_____

HOW CAN I BE BETTER TOMORROW?

_____
_____
_____
_____
_____
_____

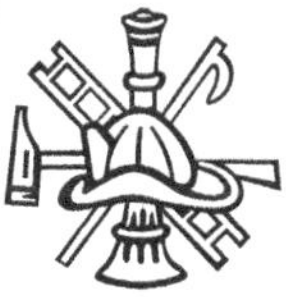

DATE: _____ CREW: _____
WEATHER: _____ _____
STATION: _____ _____
UNIT: _____ _____

WHAT WAS THE BEST PART OF MY DAY?

_____
_____
_____
_____
_____
_____

WHAT TROUBLED ME TODAY?

_____
_____
_____
_____
_____
_____

WHAT AM I GRATEFUL FOR TODAY?

_____
_____
_____
_____
_____
_____

HOW CAN I BE BETTER TOMORROW?

_____
_____
_____
_____
_____
_____

DATE: CREW:
WEATHER:
STATION:
UNIT:

WHAT WAS THE BEST PART OF MY DAY?

WHAT TROUBLED ME TODAY?

WHAT AM I GRATEFUL FOR TODAY?

HOW CAN I BE BETTER TOMORROW?

DATE: _____ CREW: _____
WEATHER: _____ _____
STATION: _____ _____
UNIT: _____ _____

WHAT WAS THE BEST PART OF MY DAY?

_____
_____
_____
_____
_____
_____

WHAT TROUBLED ME TODAY?

_____
_____
_____
_____
_____
_____

WHAT AM I GRATEFUL FOR TODAY?

_____
_____
_____
_____
_____
_____

HOW CAN I BE BETTER TOMORROW?

_____
_____
_____
_____
_____

DATE: _____ CREW: _____
WEATHER: _____ _____
STATION: _____ _____
UNIT: _____ _____

WHAT WAS THE BEST PART OF MY DAY?

_____
_____
_____
_____
_____
_____

WHAT TROUBLED ME TODAY?

_____
_____
_____
_____
_____
_____

WHAT AM I GRATEFUL FOR TODAY?

_____
_____
_____
_____
_____
_____

HOW CAN I BE BETTER TOMORROW?

_____
_____
_____
_____
_____

DATE: _____ CREW: _____
WEATHER: _____ _____
STATION: _____ _____
UNIT: _____ _____

WHAT WAS THE BEST PART OF MY DAY?

_____
_____
_____
_____
_____
_____

WHAT TROUBLED ME TODAY?

_____
_____
_____
_____
_____
_____

WHAT AM I GRATEFUL FOR TODAY?

_____
_____
_____
_____
_____
_____

HOW CAN I BE BETTER TOMORROW?

_____
_____
_____
_____
_____
_____

DATE: _____   CREW: _____
WEATHER: _____   _____
STATION: _____   _____
UNIT: _____   _____

WHAT WAS THE BEST PART OF MY DAY?

_____
_____
_____
_____
_____
_____

WHAT TROUBLED ME TODAY?

_____
_____
_____
_____
_____
_____

WHAT AM I GRATEFUL FOR TODAY?

_____
_____
_____
_____
_____
_____

HOW CAN I BE BETTER TOMORROW?

_____
_____
_____
_____
_____
_____

DATE: CREW:
WEATHER:
STATION:
UNIT:

WHAT WAS THE BEST PART OF MY DAY?

WHAT TROUBLED ME TODAY?

WHAT AM I GRATEFUL FOR TODAY?

HOW CAN I BE BETTER TOMORROW?

DATE: _____ CREW: _____
WEATHER: _____ _____
STATION: _____ _____
UNIT: _____ _____

WHAT WAS THE BEST PART OF MY DAY?

_____
_____
_____
_____
_____

WHAT TROUBLED ME TODAY?

_____
_____
_____
_____
_____

WHAT AM I GRATEFUL FOR TODAY?

_____
_____
_____
_____
_____

HOW CAN I BE BETTER TOMORROW?

_____
_____
_____
_____
_____

DATE: CREW:
WEATHER:
STATION:
UNIT:

WHAT WAS THE BEST PART OF MY DAY?

WHAT TROUBLED ME TODAY?

WHAT AM I GRATEFUL FOR TODAY?

HOW CAN I BE BETTER TOMORROW?

DATE: CREW:

WEATHER:

STATION:

UNIT:

WHAT WAS THE BEST PART OF MY DAY?

WHAT TROUBLED ME TODAY?

WHAT AM I GRATEFUL FOR TODAY?

HOW CAN I BE BETTER TOMORROW?

DATE: _____ CREW: _____
WEATHER: _____ _____
STATION: _____ _____
UNIT: _____

WHAT WAS THE BEST PART OF MY DAY?

_____
_____
_____
_____
_____
_____

WHAT TROUBLED ME TODAY?

_____
_____
_____
_____
_____
_____

WHAT AM I GRATEFUL FOR TODAY?

_____
_____
_____
_____
_____
_____

HOW CAN I BE BETTER TOMORROW?

_____
_____
_____
_____
_____
_____

DATE: _____ CREW: _____
WEATHER: _____ _____
STATION: _____
UNIT: _____

WHAT WAS THE BEST PART OF MY DAY?

_____
_____
_____
_____
_____
_____

WHAT TROUBLED ME TODAY?

_____
_____
_____
_____
_____
_____

WHAT AM I GRATEFUL FOR TODAY?

_____
_____
_____
_____
_____
_____

HOW CAN I BE BETTER TOMORROW?

_____
_____
_____
_____
_____

DATE: _____ CREW: _____
WEATHER: _____ _____
STATION: _____ _____
UNIT: _____ _____

WHAT WAS THE BEST PART OF MY DAY?

_____
_____
_____
_____
_____
_____

WHAT TROUBLED ME TODAY?

_____
_____
_____
_____
_____
_____

WHAT AM I GRATEFUL FOR TODAY?

_____
_____
_____
_____
_____
_____

HOW CAN I BE BETTER TOMORROW?

_____
_____
_____
_____
_____
_____

DATE: _____ CREW: _____
WEATHER: _____ _____
STATION: _____ _____
UNIT: _____

WHAT WAS THE BEST PART OF MY DAY?

WHAT TROUBLED ME TODAY?

WHAT AM I GRATEFUL FOR TODAY?

HOW CAN I BE BETTER TOMORROW?

DATE: _____ CREW: _____
WEATHER: _____ _____
STATION: _____ _____
UNIT: _____ _____

WHAT WAS THE BEST PART OF MY DAY?

_____
_____
_____
_____
_____
_____

WHAT TROUBLED ME TODAY?

_____
_____
_____
_____
_____
_____

WHAT AM I GRATEFUL FOR TODAY?

_____
_____
_____
_____
_____
_____

HOW CAN I BE BETTER TOMORROW?

_____
_____
_____
_____
_____
_____

DATE: _____ CREW: _____
WEATHER: _____ _____
STATION: _____ _____
UNIT: _____ _____

WHAT WAS THE BEST PART OF MY DAY?

_____
_____
_____
_____
_____
_____

WHAT TROUBLED ME TODAY?

_____
_____
_____
_____
_____
_____

WHAT AM I GRATEFUL FOR TODAY?

_____
_____
_____
_____
_____
_____

HOW CAN I BE BETTER TOMORROW?

_____
_____
_____
_____
_____
_____

DATE: _____ CREW: _____
WEATHER: _____ _____
STATION: _____ _____
UNIT: _____

WHAT WAS THE BEST PART OF MY DAY?

_____
_____
_____
_____
_____
_____

WHAT TROUBLED ME TODAY?

_____
_____
_____
_____
_____
_____

WHAT AM I GRATEFUL FOR TODAY?

_____
_____
_____
_____
_____
_____

HOW CAN I BE BETTER TOMORROW?

_____
_____
_____
_____
_____
_____

DATE: _____   CREW: _____
WEATHER: _____   _____
STATION: _____   _____
UNIT: _____   _____

WHAT WAS THE BEST PART OF MY DAY?

_____
_____
_____
_____
_____
_____

WHAT TROUBLED ME TODAY?

_____
_____
_____
_____
_____
_____

WHAT AM I GRATEFUL FOR TODAY?

_____
_____
_____
_____
_____
_____

HOW CAN I BE BETTER TOMORROW?

_____
_____
_____
_____
_____

DATE: _____ CREW: _____
WEATHER: _____ _____
STATION: _____ _____
UNIT: _____

WHAT WAS THE BEST PART OF MY DAY?

_____
_____
_____
_____
_____

WHAT TROUBLED ME TODAY?

_____
_____
_____
_____
_____

WHAT AM I GRATEFUL FOR TODAY?

_____
_____
_____
_____
_____

HOW CAN I BE BETTER TOMORROW?

_____
_____
_____
_____
_____

DATE: _____ CREW: _____
WEATHER: _____ _____
STATION: _____ _____
UNIT: _____

WHAT WAS THE BEST PART OF MY DAY?

_____
_____
_____
_____
_____

WHAT TROUBLED ME TODAY?

_____
_____
_____
_____
_____

WHAT AM I GRATEFUL FOR TODAY?

_____
_____
_____
_____
_____

HOW CAN I BE BETTER TOMORROW?

_____
_____
_____
_____
_____

DATE: _____ CREW: _____
WEATHER: _____ _____
STATION: _____ _____
UNIT: _____ _____

WHAT WAS THE BEST PART OF MY DAY?

_____
_____
_____
_____
_____
_____

WHAT TROUBLED ME TODAY?

_____
_____
_____
_____
_____
_____

WHAT AM I GRATEFUL FOR TODAY?

_____
_____
_____
_____
_____
_____

HOW CAN I BE BETTER TOMORROW?

_____
_____
_____
_____

DATE: _____ CREW: _____
WEATHER: _____ _____
STATION: _____ _____
UNIT: _____

WHAT WAS THE BEST PART OF MY DAY?

_____
_____
_____
_____
_____
_____

WHAT TROUBLED ME TODAY?

_____
_____
_____
_____
_____
_____

WHAT AM I GRATEFUL FOR TODAY?

_____
_____
_____
_____
_____
_____

HOW CAN I BE BETTER TOMORROW?

_____
_____
_____
_____
_____
_____

DATE: _____ CREW: _____
WEATHER: _____ _____
STATION: _____ _____
UNIT: _____ _____

WHAT WAS THE BEST PART OF MY DAY?

_____
_____
_____
_____
_____
_____

WHAT TROUBLED ME TODAY?

_____
_____
_____
_____
_____
_____

WHAT AM I GRATEFUL FOR TODAY?

_____
_____
_____
_____
_____
_____

HOW CAN I BE BETTER TOMORROW?

_____
_____
_____
_____
_____

DATE: _____ CREW: _____
WEATHER: _____ _____
STATION: _____ _____
UNIT: _____ _____

WHAT WAS THE BEST PART OF MY DAY?

_____
_____
_____
_____
_____

WHAT TROUBLED ME TODAY?

_____
_____
_____
_____
_____

WHAT AM I GRATEFUL FOR TODAY?

_____
_____
_____
_____
_____

HOW CAN I BE BETTER TOMORROW?

_____
_____
_____
_____

DATE: _____ CREW: _____
WEATHER: _____ _____
STATION: _____ _____
UNIT: _____ _____

WHAT WAS THE BEST PART OF MY DAY?

_____
_____
_____
_____
_____
_____

WHAT TROUBLED ME TODAY?

_____
_____
_____
_____
_____
_____

WHAT AM I GRATEFUL FOR TODAY?

_____
_____
_____
_____
_____
_____

HOW CAN I BE BETTER TOMORROW?

_____
_____
_____
_____
_____
_____

DATE: _____ CREW: _____
WEATHER: _____ _____
STATION: _____ _____
UNIT: _____ _____

WHAT WAS THE BEST PART OF MY DAY?

_____
_____
_____
_____
_____
_____

WHAT TROUBLED ME TODAY?

_____
_____
_____
_____
_____
_____

WHAT AM I GRATEFUL FOR TODAY?

_____
_____
_____
_____
_____
_____

HOW CAN I BE BETTER TOMORROW?

_____
_____
_____
_____
_____

DATE: _____ CREW: _____
WEATHER: _____ _____
STATION: _____ _____
UNIT: _____

WHAT WAS THE BEST PART OF MY DAY?

_____
_____
_____
_____
_____
_____

WHAT TROUBLED ME TODAY?

_____
_____
_____
_____
_____
_____

WHAT AM I GRATEFUL FOR TODAY?

_____
_____
_____
_____
_____
_____

HOW CAN I BE BETTER TOMORROW?

_____
_____
_____
_____
_____
_____

DATE: _____ CREW: _____
WEATHER: _____ _____
STATION: _____ _____
UNIT: _____ _____

WHAT WAS THE BEST PART OF MY DAY?

_____
_____
_____
_____
_____
_____

WHAT TROUBLED ME TODAY?

_____
_____
_____
_____
_____
_____

WHAT AM I GRATEFUL FOR TODAY?

_____
_____
_____
_____
_____
_____

HOW CAN I BE BETTER TOMORROW?

_____
_____
_____
_____
_____
_____

DATE: _____ CREW: _____
WEATHER: _____ _____
STATION: _____ _____
UNIT: _____ _____

WHAT WAS THE BEST PART OF MY DAY?

_____
_____
_____
_____
_____

WHAT TROUBLED ME TODAY?

_____
_____
_____
_____
_____

WHAT AM I GRATEFUL FOR TODAY?

_____
_____
_____
_____
_____

HOW CAN I BE BETTER TOMORROW?

_____
_____
_____
_____
_____

DATE: _____ CREW: _____
WEATHER: _____ _____
STATION: _____ _____
UNIT: _____ _____

WHAT WAS THE BEST PART OF MY DAY?

_____
_____
_____
_____
_____

WHAT TROUBLED ME TODAY?

_____
_____
_____
_____
_____

WHAT AM I GRATEFUL FOR TODAY?

_____
_____
_____
_____
_____

HOW CAN I BE BETTER TOMORROW?

_____
_____
_____
_____
_____

DATE: _____ CREW: _____
WEATHER: _____ _____
STATION: _____ _____
UNIT: _____ _____

WHAT WAS THE BEST PART OF MY DAY?

_____
_____
_____
_____
_____
_____

WHAT TROUBLED ME TODAY?

_____
_____
_____
_____
_____
_____

WHAT AM I GRATEFUL FOR TODAY?

_____
_____
_____
_____
_____
_____

HOW CAN I BE BETTER TOMORROW?

_____
_____
_____
_____
_____
_____

DATE: _____   CREW: _____
WEATHER: _____   _____
STATION: _____   _____
UNIT: _____   _____

WHAT WAS THE BEST PART OF MY DAY?

_____
_____
_____
_____
_____
_____

WHAT TROUBLED ME TODAY?

_____
_____
_____
_____
_____
_____

WHAT AM I GRATEFUL FOR TODAY?

_____
_____
_____
_____
_____
_____

HOW CAN I BE BETTER TOMORROW?

_____
_____
_____
_____
_____
_____

DATE: CREW:
WEATHER:
STATION:
UNIT:

WHAT WAS THE BEST PART OF MY DAY?

WHAT TROUBLED ME TODAY?

WHAT AM I GRATEFUL FOR TODAY?

HOW CAN I BE BETTER TOMORROW?

DATE: _____ CREW: _____
WEATHER: _____ _____
STATION: _____ _____
UNIT: _____ _____

WHAT WAS THE BEST PART OF MY DAY?

_____
_____
_____
_____
_____
_____

WHAT TROUBLED ME TODAY?

_____
_____
_____
_____
_____
_____

WHAT AM I GRATEFUL FOR TODAY?

_____
_____
_____
_____
_____
_____

HOW CAN I BE BETTER TOMORROW?

_____
_____
_____
_____
_____
_____

DATE: _____ CREW: _____
WEATHER: _____ _____
STATION: _____ _____
UNIT: _____ _____

WHAT WAS THE BEST PART OF MY DAY?

_____
_____
_____
_____
_____
_____

WHAT TROUBLED ME TODAY?

_____
_____
_____
_____
_____
_____

WHAT AM I GRATEFUL FOR TODAY?

_____
_____
_____
_____
_____
_____

HOW CAN I BE BETTER TOMORROW?

_____
_____
_____
_____
_____

DATE: CREW:

WEATHER:

STATION:

UNIT:

WHAT WAS THE BEST PART OF MY DAY?

WHAT TROUBLED ME TODAY?

WHAT AM I GRATEFUL FOR TODAY?

HOW CAN I BE BETTER TOMORROW?

DATE: _____ CREW: _____
WEATHER: _____ _____
STATION: _____ _____
UNIT: _____ _____

WHAT WAS THE BEST PART OF MY DAY?

_____
_____
_____
_____
_____

WHAT TROUBLED ME TODAY?

_____
_____
_____
_____
_____

WHAT AM I GRATEFUL FOR TODAY?

_____
_____
_____
_____
_____

HOW CAN I BE BETTER TOMORROW?

_____
_____
_____
_____
_____

DATE: _____ CREW: _____
WEATHER: _____ _____
STATION: _____ _____
UNIT: _____ _____

WHAT WAS THE BEST PART OF MY DAY?

_____
_____
_____
_____
_____
_____

WHAT TROUBLED ME TODAY?

_____
_____
_____
_____
_____
_____

WHAT AM I GRATEFUL FOR TODAY?

_____
_____
_____
_____
_____
_____

HOW CAN I BE BETTER TOMORROW?

_____
_____
_____
_____
_____
_____

DATE: _____   CREW: _____
WEATHER: _____   _____
STATION: _____   _____
UNIT: _____

WHAT WAS THE BEST PART OF MY DAY?

_____
_____
_____
_____
_____

WHAT TROUBLED ME TODAY?

_____
_____
_____
_____
_____

WHAT AM I GRATEFUL FOR TODAY?

_____
_____
_____
_____
_____

HOW CAN I BE BETTER TOMORROW?

_____
_____
_____
_____
_____

DATE: _____   CREW: _____
WEATHER: _____   _____
STATION: _____   _____
UNIT: _____   _____

WHAT WAS THE BEST PART OF MY DAY?

_____
_____
_____
_____
_____
_____

WHAT TROUBLED ME TODAY?

_____
_____
_____
_____
_____
_____

WHAT AM I GRATEFUL FOR TODAY?

_____
_____
_____
_____
_____
_____

HOW CAN I BE BETTER TOMORROW?

_____
_____
_____
_____
_____
_____

DATE: _____   CREW: _____
WEATHER: _____   _____
STATION: _____   _____
UNIT: _____   _____

WHAT WAS THE BEST PART OF MY DAY?

_____
_____
_____
_____
_____

WHAT TROUBLED ME TODAY?

_____
_____
_____
_____
_____

WHAT AM I GRATEFUL FOR TODAY?

_____
_____
_____
_____
_____

HOW CAN I BE BETTER TOMORROW?

_____
_____
_____
_____
_____

DATE: _____ CREW: _____
WEATHER: _____ _____
STATION: _____ _____
UNIT: _____

WHAT WAS THE BEST PART OF MY DAY?

_____
_____
_____
_____
_____
_____

WHAT TROUBLED ME TODAY?

_____
_____
_____
_____
_____
_____

WHAT AM I GRATEFUL FOR TODAY?

_____
_____
_____
_____
_____
_____

HOW CAN I BE BETTER TOMORROW?

_____
_____
_____
_____
_____
_____

DATE: _____ CREW: _____
WEATHER: _____ _____
STATION: _____ _____
UNIT: _____ _____

WHAT WAS THE BEST PART OF MY DAY?

_____
_____
_____
_____
_____
_____

WHAT TROUBLED ME TODAY?

_____
_____
_____
_____
_____
_____

WHAT AM I GRATEFUL FOR TODAY?

_____
_____
_____
_____
_____
_____

HOW CAN I BE BETTER TOMORROW?

_____
_____
_____
_____
_____
_____

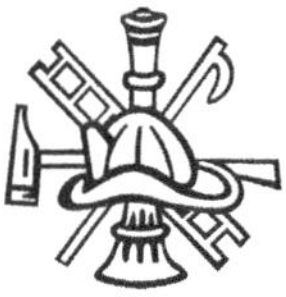

DATE: _____   CREW: _____
WEATHER: _____   _____
STATION: _____   _____
UNIT: _____   _____

WHAT WAS THE BEST PART OF MY DAY?

_____
_____
_____
_____
_____
_____

WHAT TROUBLED ME TODAY?

_____
_____
_____
_____
_____
_____

WHAT AM I GRATEFUL FOR TODAY?

_____
_____
_____
_____
_____
_____

HOW CAN I BE BETTER TOMORROW?

_____
_____
_____
_____
_____
_____

DATE: CREW:
WEATHER:
STATION:
UNIT:

WHAT WAS THE BEST PART OF MY DAY?

WHAT TROUBLED ME TODAY?

WHAT AM I GRATEFUL FOR TODAY?

HOW CAN I BE BETTER TOMORROW?

DATE: CREW:
WEATHER:
STATION:
UNIT:

WHAT WAS THE BEST PART OF MY DAY?

WHAT TROUBLED ME TODAY?

WHAT AM I GRATEFUL FOR TODAY?

HOW CAN I BE BETTER TOMORROW?

DATE: _____ CREW: _____
WEATHER: _____ _____
STATION: _____ _____
UNIT: _____ _____

WHAT WAS THE BEST PART OF MY DAY?

_____
_____
_____
_____
_____
_____
_____

WHAT TROUBLED ME TODAY?

_____
_____
_____
_____
_____
_____
_____

WHAT AM I GRATEFUL FOR TODAY?

_____
_____
_____
_____
_____
_____
_____

HOW CAN I BE BETTER TOMORROW?

_____
_____
_____
_____
_____
_____

DATE: CREW:

WEATHER:

STATION:

UNIT:

WHAT WAS THE BEST PART OF MY DAY?

WHAT TROUBLED ME TODAY?

WHAT AM I GRATEFUL FOR TODAY?

HOW CAN I BE BETTER TOMORROW?

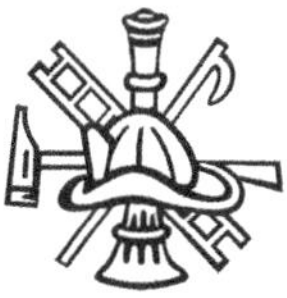

DATE: _____ CREW: _____
WEATHER: _____ _____
STATION: _____ _____
UNIT: _____ _____

WHAT WAS THE BEST PART OF MY DAY?

_____
_____
_____
_____
_____

WHAT TROUBLED ME TODAY?

_____
_____
_____
_____
_____

WHAT AM I GRATEFUL FOR TODAY?

_____
_____
_____
_____
_____

HOW CAN I BE BETTER TOMORROW?

_____
_____
_____
_____
_____

DATE: _____ CREW: _____
WEATHER: _____ _____
STATION: _____ _____
UNIT: _____ _____

WHAT WAS THE BEST PART OF MY DAY?

_____
_____
_____
_____
_____
_____

WHAT TROUBLED ME TODAY?

_____
_____
_____
_____
_____
_____

WHAT AM I GRATEFUL FOR TODAY?

_____
_____
_____
_____
_____
_____

HOW CAN I BE BETTER TOMORROW?

_____
_____
_____
_____
_____

DATE: _____ CREW: _____
WEATHER: _____ _____
STATION: _____ _____
UNIT: _____

WHAT WAS THE BEST PART OF MY DAY?

_____
_____
_____
_____
_____

WHAT TROUBLED ME TODAY?

_____
_____
_____
_____
_____

WHAT AM I GRATEFUL FOR TODAY?

_____
_____
_____
_____
_____

HOW CAN I BE BETTER TOMORROW?

_____
_____
_____
_____
_____

DATE: _____ CREW: _____
WEATHER: _____ _____
STATION: _____ _____
UNIT: _____ _____

WHAT WAS THE BEST PART OF MY DAY?

_____
_____
_____
_____
_____
_____

WHAT TROUBLED ME TODAY?

_____
_____
_____
_____
_____
_____

WHAT AM I GRATEFUL FOR TODAY?

_____
_____
_____
_____
_____
_____

HOW CAN I BE BETTER TOMORROW?

_____
_____
_____
_____
_____
_____

DATE: _____ CREW: _____
WEATHER: _____ _____
STATION: _____ _____
UNIT: _____ _____

WHAT WAS THE BEST PART OF MY DAY?

_____
_____
_____
_____
_____
_____

WHAT TROUBLED ME TODAY?

_____
_____
_____
_____
_____
_____

WHAT AM I GRATEFUL FOR TODAY?

_____
_____
_____
_____
_____
_____

HOW CAN I BE BETTER TOMORROW?

_____
_____
_____
_____
_____
_____

DATE: CREW:
WEATHER:
STATION:
UNIT:

WHAT WAS THE BEST PART OF MY DAY?

WHAT TROUBLED ME TODAY?

WHAT AM I GRATEFUL FOR TODAY?

HOW CAN I BE BETTER TOMORROW?

DATE: _____ CREW: _____
WEATHER: _____ _____
STATION: _____ _____
UNIT: _____ _____

WHAT WAS THE BEST PART OF MY DAY?

_____
_____
_____
_____
_____
_____

WHAT TROUBLED ME TODAY?

_____
_____
_____
_____
_____
_____

WHAT AM I GRATEFUL FOR TODAY?

_____
_____
_____
_____
_____
_____

HOW CAN I BE BETTER TOMORROW?

_____
_____
_____
_____
_____
_____

DATE: _____ CREW: _____
WEATHER: _____ _____
STATION: _____ _____
UNIT: _____ _____

WHAT WAS THE BEST PART OF MY DAY?

_____
_____
_____
_____
_____
_____

WHAT TROUBLED ME TODAY?

_____
_____
_____
_____
_____
_____

WHAT AM I GRATEFUL FOR TODAY?

_____
_____
_____
_____
_____
_____

HOW CAN I BE BETTER TOMORROW?

_____
_____
_____
_____
_____
_____

DATE: CREW:

WEATHER:

STATION:

UNIT:

WHAT WAS THE BEST PART OF MY DAY?

WHAT TROUBLED ME TODAY?

WHAT AM I GRATEFUL FOR TODAY?

HOW CAN I BE BETTER TOMORROW?

DATE: _____   CREW: _____
WEATHER: _____   _____
STATION: _____   _____
UNIT: _____   _____

WHAT WAS THE BEST PART OF MY DAY?

_____
_____
_____
_____
_____
_____

WHAT TROUBLED ME TODAY?

_____
_____
_____
_____
_____
_____

WHAT AM I GRATEFUL FOR TODAY?

_____
_____
_____
_____
_____
_____

HOW CAN I BE BETTER TOMORROW?

_____
_____
_____
_____
_____
_____

DATE: _____ CREW: _____
WEATHER: _____ _____
STATION: _____ _____
UNIT: _____ _____

WHAT WAS THE BEST PART OF MY DAY?

_____
_____
_____
_____
_____
_____

WHAT TROUBLED ME TODAY?

_____
_____
_____
_____
_____
_____

WHAT AM I GRATEFUL FOR TODAY?

_____
_____
_____
_____
_____
_____

HOW CAN I BE BETTER TOMORROW?

_____
_____
_____
_____
_____
_____

DATE: _____ CREW: _____
WEATHER: _____ _____
STATION: _____ _____
UNIT: _____ _____

WHAT WAS THE BEST PART OF MY DAY?

_____
_____
_____
_____
_____

WHAT TROUBLED ME TODAY?

_____
_____
_____
_____
_____

WHAT AM I GRATEFUL FOR TODAY?

_____
_____
_____
_____
_____

HOW CAN I BE BETTER TOMORROW?

_____
_____
_____
_____
_____

DATE: _____ CREW: _____
WEATHER: _____ _____
STATION: _____ _____
UNIT: _____ _____

WHAT WAS THE BEST PART OF MY DAY?

_____
_____
_____
_____
_____

WHAT TROUBLED ME TODAY?

_____
_____
_____
_____
_____

WHAT AM I GRATEFUL FOR TODAY?

_____
_____
_____
_____
_____

HOW CAN I BE BETTER TOMORROW?

_____
_____
_____
_____
_____

DATE: _____   CREW: _____
WEATHER: _____   _____
STATION: _____   _____
UNIT: _____   _____

WHAT WAS THE BEST PART OF MY DAY?

_____
_____
_____
_____
_____
_____

WHAT TROUBLED ME TODAY?

_____
_____
_____
_____
_____
_____

WHAT AM I GRATEFUL FOR TODAY?

_____
_____
_____
_____
_____
_____

HOW CAN I BE BETTER TOMORROW?

_____
_____
_____
_____
_____
_____

DATE: CREW:

WEATHER:

STATION:

UNIT:

WHAT WAS THE BEST PART OF MY DAY?

WHAT TROUBLED ME TODAY?

WHAT AM I GRATEFUL FOR TODAY?

HOW CAN I BE BETTER TOMORROW?

DATE: _____ CREW: _____
WEATHER: _____ _____
STATION: _____
UNIT: _____

WHAT WAS THE BEST PART OF MY DAY?

_____
_____
_____
_____
_____
_____

WHAT TROUBLED ME TODAY?

_____
_____
_____
_____
_____
_____

WHAT AM I GRATEFUL FOR TODAY?

_____
_____
_____
_____
_____
_____

HOW CAN I BE BETTER TOMORROW?

_____
_____
_____
_____
_____
_____

DATE: _____ CREW: _____
WEATHER: _____ _____
STATION: _____ _____
UNIT: _____ _____

WHAT WAS THE BEST PART OF MY DAY?

_____
_____
_____
_____
_____
_____

WHAT TROUBLED ME TODAY?

_____
_____
_____
_____
_____
_____

WHAT AM I GRATEFUL FOR TODAY?

_____
_____
_____
_____
_____
_____

HOW CAN I BE BETTER TOMORROW?

_____
_____
_____
_____
_____
_____

DATE: CREW:
WEATHER:
STATION:
UNIT:

WHAT WAS THE BEST PART OF MY DAY?

WHAT TROUBLED ME TODAY?

WHAT AM I GRATEFUL FOR TODAY?

HOW CAN I BE BETTER TOMORROW?

DATE: _____ CREW: _____
WEATHER: _____ _____
STATION: _____ _____
UNIT: _____ _____

WHAT WAS THE BEST PART OF MY DAY?

_____
_____
_____
_____
_____
_____

WHAT TROUBLED ME TODAY?

_____
_____
_____
_____
_____
_____

WHAT AM I GRATEFUL FOR TODAY?

_____
_____
_____
_____
_____
_____

HOW CAN I BE BETTER TOMORROW?

_____
_____
_____
_____
_____
_____

DATE: _____ CREW: _____
WEATHER: _____ _____
STATION: _____ _____
UNIT: _____ _____

WHAT WAS THE BEST PART OF MY DAY?

_____
_____
_____
_____
_____
_____

WHAT TROUBLED ME TODAY?

_____
_____
_____
_____
_____
_____

WHAT AM I GRATEFUL FOR TODAY?

_____
_____
_____
_____
_____
_____

HOW CAN I BE BETTER TOMORROW?

_____
_____
_____
_____
_____
_____

DATE: _____ CREW: _____
WEATHER: _____ _____
STATION: _____ _____
UNIT: _____ _____

WHAT WAS THE BEST PART OF MY DAY?

_____
_____
_____
_____
_____
_____

WHAT TROUBLED ME TODAY?

_____
_____
_____
_____
_____
_____
_____

WHAT AM I GRATEFUL FOR TODAY?

_____
_____
_____
_____
_____
_____
_____

HOW CAN I BE BETTER TOMORROW?

_____
_____
_____
_____
_____

DATE: _____ CREW: _____
WEATHER: _____ _____
STATION: _____ _____
UNIT: _____ _____

WHAT WAS THE BEST PART OF MY DAY?

_____
_____
_____
_____
_____

WHAT TROUBLED ME TODAY?

_____
_____
_____
_____
_____

WHAT AM I GRATEFUL FOR TODAY?

_____
_____
_____
_____
_____

HOW CAN I BE BETTER TOMORROW?

_____
_____
_____
_____
_____

DATE: _____ CREW: _____
WEATHER: _____ _____
STATION: _____ _____
UNIT: _____ _____

WHAT WAS THE BEST PART OF MY DAY?

_____
_____
_____
_____
_____
_____

WHAT TROUBLED ME TODAY?

_____
_____
_____
_____
_____
_____

WHAT AM I GRATEFUL FOR TODAY?

_____
_____
_____
_____
_____
_____

HOW CAN I BE BETTER TOMORROW?

_____
_____
_____
_____
_____

DATE: _____ CREW: _____
WEATHER: _____ _____
STATION: _____ _____
UNIT: _____

WHAT WAS THE BEST PART OF MY DAY?

_____
_____
_____
_____
_____

WHAT TROUBLED ME TODAY?

_____
_____
_____
_____
_____

WHAT AM I GRATEFUL FOR TODAY?

_____
_____
_____
_____
_____

HOW CAN I BE BETTER TOMORROW?

_____
_____
_____
_____
_____

DATE: CREW:
WEATHER:
STATION:
UNIT:

WHAT WAS THE BEST PART OF MY DAY?

WHAT TROUBLED ME TODAY?

WHAT AM I GRATEFUL FOR TODAY?

HOW CAN I BE BETTER TOMORROW?

DATE: _____ CREW: _____
WEATHER: _____ _____
STATION: _____ _____
UNIT: _____ _____

WHAT WAS THE BEST PART OF MY DAY?

_____
_____
_____
_____
_____
_____

WHAT TROUBLED ME TODAY?

_____
_____
_____
_____
_____
_____

WHAT AM I GRATEFUL FOR TODAY?

_____
_____
_____
_____
_____
_____

HOW CAN I BE BETTER TOMORROW?

_____
_____
_____
_____
_____
_____

DATE: CREW:

WEATHER:

STATION:

UNIT:

WHAT WAS THE BEST PART OF MY DAY?

WHAT TROUBLED ME TODAY?

WHAT AM I GRATEFUL FOR TODAY?

HOW CAN I BE BETTER TOMORROW?

DATE: CREW:
WEATHER:
STATION:
UNIT:

WHAT WAS THE BEST PART OF MY DAY?

WHAT TROUBLED ME TODAY?

WHAT AM I GRATEFUL FOR TODAY?

HOW CAN I BE BETTER TOMORROW?

DATE: CREW:
WEATHER:
STATION:
UNIT:

WHAT WAS THE BEST PART OF MY DAY?

WHAT TROUBLED ME TODAY?

WHAT AM I GRATEFUL FOR TODAY?

HOW CAN I BE BETTER TOMORROW?

DATE: _____ CREW: _____
WEATHER: _____ _____
STATION: _____ _____
UNIT: _____ _____

WHAT WAS THE BEST PART OF MY DAY?

_____
_____
_____
_____
_____
_____

WHAT TROUBLED ME TODAY?

_____
_____
_____
_____
_____
_____

WHAT AM I GRATEFUL FOR TODAY?

_____
_____
_____
_____
_____
_____

HOW CAN I BE BETTER TOMORROW?

_____
_____
_____
_____
_____
_____

DATE: CREW:

WEATHER:

STATION:

UNIT:

WHAT WAS THE BEST PART OF MY DAY?

WHAT TROUBLED ME TODAY?

WHAT AM I GRATEFUL FOR TODAY?

HOW CAN I BE BETTER TOMORROW?

DATE: CREW:

WEATHER:

STATION:

UNIT:

WHAT WAS THE BEST PART OF MY DAY?

WHAT TROUBLED ME TODAY?

WHAT AM I GRATEFUL FOR TODAY?

HOW CAN I BE BETTER TOMORROW?

DATE: _____ CREW: _____
WEATHER: _____ _____
STATION: _____ _____
UNIT: _____ _____

WHAT WAS THE BEST PART OF MY DAY?

_____
_____
_____
_____
_____
_____

WHAT TROUBLED ME TODAY?

_____
_____
_____
_____
_____
_____

WHAT AM I GRATEFUL FOR TODAY?

_____
_____
_____
_____
_____
_____

HOW CAN I BE BETTER TOMORROW?

_____
_____
_____
_____
_____
_____

DATE: _____   CREW: _____
WEATHER: _____   _____
STATION: _____   _____
UNIT: _____

WHAT WAS THE BEST PART OF MY DAY?

_____
_____
_____
_____
_____
_____

WHAT TROUBLED ME TODAY?

_____
_____
_____
_____
_____
_____

WHAT AM I GRATEFUL FOR TODAY?

_____
_____
_____
_____
_____
_____

HOW CAN I BE BETTER TOMORROW?

_____
_____
_____
_____
_____
_____

DATE: CREW:
WEATHER:
STATION:
UNIT:

WHAT WAS THE BEST PART OF MY DAY?

WHAT TROUBLED ME TODAY?

WHAT AM I GRATEFUL FOR TODAY?

HOW CAN I BE BETTER TOMORROW?

DATE: _____ CREW: _____
WEATHER: _____ _____
STATION: _____ _____
UNIT: _____

WHAT WAS THE BEST PART OF MY DAY?

_____
_____
_____
_____
_____

WHAT TROUBLED ME TODAY?

_____
_____
_____
_____
_____

WHAT AM I GRATEFUL FOR TODAY?

_____
_____
_____
_____
_____

HOW CAN I BE BETTER TOMORROW?

_____
_____
_____
_____
_____

DATE: _____ CREW: _____
WEATHER: _____ _____
STATION: _____ _____
UNIT: _____ _____

WHAT WAS THE BEST PART OF MY DAY?

_____
_____
_____
_____
_____
_____

WHAT TROUBLED ME TODAY?

_____
_____
_____
_____
_____
_____

WHAT AM I GRATEFUL FOR TODAY?

_____
_____
_____
_____
_____
_____

HOW CAN I BE BETTER TOMORROW?

_____
_____
_____
_____
_____
_____

DATE: _____ CREW: _____
WEATHER: _____ _____
STATION: _____ _____
UNIT: _____ _____

WHAT WAS THE BEST PART OF MY DAY?

_____
_____
_____
_____
_____
_____

WHAT TROUBLED ME TODAY?

_____
_____
_____
_____
_____
_____

WHAT AM I GRATEFUL FOR TODAY?

_____
_____
_____
_____
_____
_____

HOW CAN I BE BETTER TOMORROW?

_____
_____
_____
_____
_____
_____

DATE: _____ CREW: _____
WEATHER: _____ _____
STATION: _____ _____
UNIT: _____ _____

WHAT WAS THE BEST PART OF MY DAY?

_____
_____
_____
_____
_____

WHAT TROUBLED ME TODAY?

_____
_____
_____
_____
_____

WHAT AM I GRATEFUL FOR TODAY?

_____
_____
_____
_____
_____

HOW CAN I BE BETTER TOMORROW?

_____
_____
_____
_____
_____

DATE: _____ CREW: _____
WEATHER: _____ _____
STATION: _____ _____
UNIT: _____

WHAT WAS THE BEST PART OF MY DAY?

_____
_____
_____
_____
_____
_____

WHAT TROUBLED ME TODAY?

_____
_____
_____
_____
_____
_____

WHAT AM I GRATEFUL FOR TODAY?

_____
_____
_____
_____
_____
_____

HOW CAN I BE BETTER TOMORROW?

_____
_____
_____
_____
_____
_____

DATE: _____ CREW: _____
WEATHER: _____ _____
STATION: _____ _____
UNIT: _____ _____

WHAT WAS THE BEST PART OF MY DAY?

_____
_____
_____
_____
_____
_____

WHAT TROUBLED ME TODAY?

_____
_____
_____
_____
_____
_____

WHAT AM I GRATEFUL FOR TODAY?

_____
_____
_____
_____
_____
_____

HOW CAN I BE BETTER TOMORROW?

_____
_____
_____
_____
_____

DATE: _____ CREW: _____
WEATHER: _____ _____
STATION: _____ _____
UNIT: _____

WHAT WAS THE BEST PART OF MY DAY?

_____
_____
_____
_____
_____
_____

WHAT TROUBLED ME TODAY?

_____
_____
_____
_____
_____
_____

WHAT AM I GRATEFUL FOR TODAY?

_____
_____
_____
_____
_____
_____

HOW CAN I BE BETTER TOMORROW?

_____
_____
_____
_____
_____
_____

DATE: _____ CREW: _____
WEATHER: _____ _____
STATION: _____ _____
UNIT: _____ _____

WHAT WAS THE BEST PART OF MY DAY?

_____
_____
_____
_____
_____
_____

WHAT TROUBLED ME TODAY?

_____
_____
_____
_____
_____
_____

WHAT AM I GRATEFUL FOR TODAY?

_____
_____
_____
_____
_____
_____

HOW CAN I BE BETTER TOMORROW?

_____
_____
_____
_____
_____
_____

DATE: _____ CREW: _____
WEATHER: _____ _____
STATION: _____ _____
UNIT: _____ _____

WHAT WAS THE BEST PART OF MY DAY?

WHAT TROUBLED ME TODAY?

WHAT AM I GRATEFUL FOR TODAY?

HOW CAN I BE BETTER TOMORROW?

DATE: _____ CREW: _____
WEATHER: _____ _____
STATION: _____ _____
UNIT: _____

WHAT WAS THE BEST PART OF MY DAY?

_____
_____
_____
_____
_____

WHAT TROUBLED ME TODAY?

_____
_____
_____
_____
_____

WHAT AM I GRATEFUL FOR TODAY?

_____
_____
_____
_____
_____

HOW CAN I BE BETTER TOMORROW?

_____
_____
_____
_____
_____

Made in the USA
Monee, IL
06 June 2023

35345778R00118